African American Wisdom

For Rachael, Moriah, Nicole,
Sarah Ann, and Christina

African American Wisdom

Selected and with
an Introduction
by
REGINALD MCKNIGHT

THE CLASSIC WISDOM COLLECTION
NEW WORLD LIBRARY
SAN RAFAEL, CALIFORNIA

The Classic Wisdom Collection
Published by New World Library
58 Paul Drive, San Rafael, CA 94903

Cover design: Greg Wittrock
Text design: Nancy Benedict
Typography: TBH Typecast, Inc.

Library of Congress Cataloging-in-Publication Data

African American wisdom / edited by Reginald Mcknight.
     p. cm. — (The Classic wisdom collection)
  Includes bibliographical references and index.
  ISBN 1-880032-34-1 (alk. paper) : $12.95
   1. Quotations, English. 2. Afro-American — Quotations.
 I. Mcknight, Reginald, 1956– .   II. Series.
PN6081.3.A37 1993
081'.08996073 — dc20   93-33729
                       CIP

First printing, February 1994
ISBN 1-880032-34-1
Printed in the U.S.A. on acid-free paper
Distributed by Publishers Group West

10 9 8 7 6 5 4 3 2 1

Contents

Publisher's Preface

Life is an endless cycle of change. We and our world will never remain the same.

Every generation has difficulty relating to the previous generation; even the language changes. The child speaks a different language than the parent.

It seems almost miraculous, then, that certain voices, certain books, are able to speak to not only one, but many generations beyond them. The plays and poems of William Shakespeare are still relevant today — still capable of giving us goose bumps, still entertaining, disturbing, and profound. Shakespeare is the writer who, in the English language, defines the word *classic*.

There are many other writers and thinkers who, for a great many reasons, can be considered classic, for they withstand the test of time. We want to present the best of them to you in the New World Library Classic Wisdom Collection, the thinkers who, even though they lived many years ago, are still relevant and important in today's world for the enduring words of wisdom they created, words that should forever be kept in print.

African American Wisdom is a special book in this collection, an eclectic gathering of the writings and spoken words of African Americans, past and present. We are proud to present this tribute to the profundity and power of African Americans.

Marc Allen
New World Library

Introduction

There is no way to squeeze nearly four hundred years of the wisdom of any one people into such a slender volume as this. This is not a distillation, not a cross section, not even an adequate sample of the wisdom of Afro-America. Everything about this compilation is more or less arbitrary, personal, probably highly idiosyncratic, for the more deeply I have delved into the realm of wisdom, the less I am able to determine exactly what wisdom is. It is likely that any dictionary would tell us that wisdom is common sense, the acquisition of knowledge, a deep and meaningful understanding of right from wrong, good and evil, which is gained through study, or experience, or both. As with all abstract words — faith, goodness, happiness, love — the word wisdom has no core meaning; it cannot be broken down to quantifiable essences and elements. Nothing can, really, neither the abstract nor the concrete. Wisdom, like any word or thing, is a kind of energy, transitory, ephemeral, contextual. We are affected by it, of course, but we never fully grasp it.

The Bible tells us that the beginning of wisdom is the fear of God. Horace says that "to have got rid of folly is the beginning of wisdom." Gustave Flaubert told George Sand some one-hundred-twenty-odd years ago that the beginning of wisdom is to be found in the hatred of the bourgeois, and I believe it was Bertrand Russell who insisted that to conquer fear is the beginning of wisdom. Thus, from four respectable, if not redoubtable, sources we learn that wisdom is both to fear and not to fear, and that wisdom is to hate and to eschew. Two plainly contradict each other; the other two may unsettle us because they seem so negative, and most of us, I dare say, tend to think of wisdom as having wholly affirmative characteristics.

If I were less patient, and perhaps less wise, I would conclude, simply, that what you see is what you get, and be done with it, or be like the college freshman, who having tried either philosophy or LSD (or both) for the first time, hysterically concludes that he does not exist and drops out.

Yet something in the way we regard the word compels me, beckons me. Most cultures have a word that is closely equivalent to the word wisdom. Most of the people I know revere those who are said to possess even the merest hint of it. "Wisdom," says the book of Proverbs, "is the principle thing; therefore get wisdom: and with all thy getting get understanding" (4:7). The Greek motto *philosophia biou kunernetes*, whose initials are Phi Beta Kappa, means "Wisdom is the guide of life." The book of Job tells us that, "The price of wisdom is above rubies" (28:18), and although the Akan tell us that "wisdom is not bought," we know, in fact, that it is. It is paid for with strife, pain, travail — traded measure for measure with our innocence. "In much wisdom is much grief," says Koheleth, author of the book of Ecclesiastes, "and she that increases knowledge increases sorrow" (1:18).

And we must remain mindful that the mere acquisition of years does not necessarily bring us wisdom. Most of us are familiar with the proverb, "There's no fool like an old fool," and history has revealed that American critic and editor H.L. Mencken was right about himself when he said, "The older I grow the more I distrust the familiar doctrine that age brings wisdom." Mencken, author of *Prejudices*, we have come to learn in recent years, was a bigot. No, it is not age, but pain that brings us wisdom. And though there is not one of us who, scuttling between earth and sky for our all-too-brief time, doesn't know pain, there is no guarantee we will leave this world wise. It all depends. "[O]ne man's wisdom is another man's folly," says Ralph Waldo Emerson, and while I may have merely *suspected* that before compiling and editing the following passages, now, afterwards, I know it's true.

It doesn't take wisdom to know that black America has had them some pain. Read two or three pages of the biography of nearly any noted or notable African American and you will know this. Visit for five minutes any predominantly black community in any American city — north St. Louis, Harlem, Compton, Woodlawn, Central Detroit, Pittsburgh's Homewood — and you'll see you some pain. But from that pain, rising like the Phoenix from its own smoking ashes, is a wisdom so bright and resplendent that you'll need your shades to behold it. Yet, if all that could be referred to as African American wisdom were a mountain, this slender volume would have to be likened to but a teaspoon of that mountain's rich black soil.

There are literally hundreds of voices, thousands of excerpts I could not use for one reason or another. And I have discovered that one could easily devote one's entire adult life to researching and collecting such works. And as I said at the beginning of this introduction the contents of this volume are, doubtless, personal, arbitrary, and idiosyncratic, yet I must say that not everything herein is something that I know beyond doubt to be necessarily wise, for though I can see the penumbra of wisdom about each and every excerpt, not all of them are an expression of my experience, pain with which I am acquainted. What is likely to be wisdom to me may very well be folly to you.

Reginald McKnight
St. Louis, Missouri, 1994

1

Do You Remember the Time?

HISTORY

My great-grandmama told my grandmama the part she lived through that my grandmama didn't live through and my grandmama told my mama what they both lived through and my mama told me what they all lived through and we were suppose to pass it down like that from generation to generation so we'd never forget.

GAYL JONES, 1975

For Africa to me . . . is more than a glamorous fact. It is a historical truth. No man can know where he is going unless he knows exactly where he has been and exactly how he arrived at his present place.

MAYA ANGELOU, 1972

What goes around comes around.

ANONYMOUS, Virginia

Exhaust the little moment. Soon it dies.
And be it gash or gold it will not come
Again in this identical disguise.

GWENDOLYN BROOKS
Exhaust the Little Moment, 1949

Day's short as ever, time's long as it has been.

ANONYMOUS, Deep South

For I am my mother's daughter, and the drums of Africa still beat in my heart. They will not let me rest while there is a single Negro boy or girl without a chance to prove his worth.

MARY MCLEOD BETHUNE, 1941

Don't forget where you came from.

ANONYMOUS, Buffalo, NY

Although I understand that I am a biological and cultural fragment of Africans, Europeans, and Native Americans, I have no problem with *wholeness* due to being made of fragments. That's because I perceive the axis of my being to be the human essence, not the ethnic or racial essence. Those first generations of my African ancestors, who experienced fragmentation and dispossession, were self-sacrificing and philosophical enough to frame a legacy for me (us) upon which we could establish and maintain a sense of wholeness and human integrity while under siege. If we're too foolish to use the sacrifices that they turned into a legacy of wisdom for sustaining our wholeness, a legacy passed on in the spirituals, the folktales, the blues, jazz, gospel and all — then that's our fault! It's our fault if we opt for nothingness after all the torment and hell those earlier generations went through.

ERSKINE PETERS, 1992

CHAPTER ONE

It would seem, at this point in our history, African Americans can calm the warring identities in our consciousness. Assimilation is not a one-way street. It's a boulevard with multiple lanes of traffic, flowing two ways, intercut by persistent jaywalkers. But our trucks are so big we've been jamming the boulevard for decades. If we understand that, especially our young people, then we have the consciousness to engage, with confidence, in the political struggle . . . to assert the authority of our claim: We are central to the notion of American identity.

ITABARI NJERI, 1993

What goes under the devil's back has to come under his belly.

ANONYMOUS, Deep South

There is no reason to repeat bad history.

ELEANOR HOLMES NORTON, 1970

For God's sake, you men and women who have been keeping yourselves away from the people

4

of your own African race, cease the ignorance; unite your hands and hearts with the people Afric, and let us reach out to the highest idealism that there is in living. . . . Sons and daughters of Africa, I say to you arise, take on the toga of race pride and throw off the brand of ignominy which has kept you back for so many centuries. Dash asunder the petty prejudices within your own fold; set at defiance the scornful designation of "nigger" uttered even by yourselves, and be a Negro in the light of the Pharaohs of Egypt, Simons of Cyrene, Hannibals of Carthage, L'Ouvertures and Dessalines of Hayti, Bydens, Barclays and Johnsons of Liberia, Lewises of Sierra Leone, and Douglass's and Du Bois's, who have made, and are making history for the race, though depreciated and in many cases unwritten. . . . To study the history of the Negro is to go back into a primitive civilization that teems with the brightest and best in art and the sciences.

MARCUS GARVEY, 1914

There is a spirit and a need and a man at the beginning of every great human advance. Each of

5

these must be right for the particular moment of history, or nothing happens.

CORETTA SCOTT KING, 1969

While I was sleeping in my bed there, things were happening in this world that directly concerned me — nobody asked me, consulted me — they just went out and did things — and changed my life.

LORRAINE HANSBERRY
Raisin in the Sun, 1959

2

Yearnin' Learnin'

KNOWLEDGE, MATURITY, EDUCATION

She said that I must always be intolerant of ignorance but understanding of illiteracy. That some people, unable to go to school, were more educated and even more intelligent than college professors. She encouraged me to listen carefully to what people called mother wit. That in those homely sayings was couched the collective wisdom of generations.

MAYA ANGELOU, 1969

A new broom sweeps clean, but an old brush knows the corners.

ANONYMOUS, North Carolina

[D]iscipline must emanate from moral authority rather than military authority. In other words, one should not be disciplined because of a threat of death or the threat of jail. One should become disciplined and appreciate the significance of it. If you are going to run for the Olympics to get a gold medal, you must run, and train, and discipline yourself, not because somebody's going to shoot you, but because your competition is going to defeat you.

JESSE JACKSON, 1981

Cunnin' better than strong.

ANONYMOUS, Creole

Herein lies the tragedy of the age: not that men are poor — all men know something of poverty; not that men are wicked — who is good? Not that men are ignorant — what is truth? Nay, but that men know so little of men.

W.E.B. DU BOIS, 1903

There's a period of life when we swallow a knowledge of ourselves and it becomes either good or sour inside.

PEARL BAILEY, 1966

She is old now. Once she was young, not long ago, really. Only a few days, it would seem. A few sunsets, a few sunrises, a few childbirths, a few deaths. But she has been old for some time now. This she knows; this she feels; this she hates. When she was young, younger, so full of life and living, so impatient for tomorrow, so hopeful of hope, she did not reckon she would be old for so long.

RANDALL KENAN, 1989

Don't look back. Something may be gaining on you.

SATCHEL [LEROY] PAIGE, 1953

We real cool. We
Left school. We

Lurk late. We
Strike straight. We
Sing sin. We
Thin gin. We
Jazz June. We
Die soon.

GWENDOLYN BROOKS
We Real Cool, 1960

A nation cannot teach its youths to think in terms of destruction and oppression without brutalizing and blunting the tender conscience and sense of justice of the youths of that country. More and more we must learn to think not in terms of race or color or language or religion or of political boundaries, but in terms of humanity. Above all races and political boundaries there is humanity. That should be considered first; and in proportion as we teach our youths of this country to love all races and all nations, we are rendering the highest service which education can render.

BOOKER T. WASHINGTON, 1913

Now if you go to libraries . . . and you read, suddenly you are closer to being liberated than you ever can be. It is only an education that liberates. Education helps one cease being intimidated by strange situations. Once you have it in your mind, you can go anywhere. . . . Read. Find that there is nothing that is not human, that if a human being can do the worst thing, it means too that a human being can do the greatest. He or she can actually dare to dream a great dream! And really create a masterpiece.

If a human being did it, then obviously I have that capability of doing it. And so do you.

MAYA ANGELOU, 1981

It's more power in being a book than a bookend.

ANONYMOUS, Colorado

When we live outside ourselves, and by that I mean on external directives only rather than from our internal knowledge and needs, when we move away from those erotic guides and within ourselves, and then our lives are limited by external and alien forms, and we conform to the needs of a structure that is not based on human need, let alone an individual's. But when we begin to live from within *outward*, in touch with the power of the erotic within ourselves, and allowing the power to inform and illuminate our actions upon the world around us, then we begin to be responsible to ourselves in the deepest sense. For as we begin to realize our deepest feelings, we begin to give up, of necessity, being satisfied with suffering and self-negation, and with the numbness which so often seems like their only alternative in our society. Our acts against oppression become integral with self, motivated and empowered from within.

AUDRE LORD, 1992

Ol' Rabbit think experience cost too much when you get it from a trap.

ANONYMOUS

The science, the art, the literature that fails to reach down and bring the humblest up to the fullest enjoyment of the blessings of our government is weak, no matter how costly the buildings or the apparatus used, or how modern the methods in instruction employed. The study of arithmetic that does not result in making someone more honest and self-reliant is defective. The study of history that does not result in making men conscientious in receiving and counting the ballots of their fellow men is most faulty. The study of art that does not result in making the strong less willing to oppress the weak means little . . . usefulness [and] service to our brother, is the supreme end of education.

BOOKER T. WASHINGTON, 1896

The bait is worth more than the fish.

ANONYMOUS, North Carolina

People like definite decisions,
Tidy answers, all the little ravelings
Snipped off, the lint removed, they
Hop happily among their roughs
Calling what they can't clutch insanity
Or saintliness

GWENDOLYN BROOKS
Memorial to Ed Bland, 1949

If you don't know much, you can't do much.

ANONYMOUS, Buffalo, NY

The old Sheep wonder where the yarn sock come from.

ANONYMOUS, 19th Century

Late comes early.

ANONYMOUS, Colorado

3

It's a Thin Line Between . . .

LOVE AND HATE

The price of hating other human beings is loving oneself less.

ELDRIDGE CLEAVER

You know, I've had a lot of experience loving my enemies — I've been thrown in jail and beaten up and I never lost my temper with the Ku Klux Klan. The problem is that I have lost my temper with my wife, I have lost my temper with my mother, I have lost my temper with my twelve-year-old son — but ultimately the problems that we talk about on a macroeconomic level or on a global level, all come back to the human level where we begin to learn to love one another at home, and in families and in one-to-one relationships; where we begin to appreciate those differences, where we begin to develop partnerships.

ANDREW YOUNG, 1985

Hatred, which could destroy so much, never failed to destroy the man who hated and this is an immutable law.

JAMES BALDWIN

Love is the most durable power in the world. . . . Love is the only force capable of transforming an enemy into a friend.

MARTIN LUTHER KING JR.

Hatred and bitterness can never cure the disease of fear, only love can do that. Hatred paralyzes life; love releases it. Hatred confuses life; love harmonizes it. Hatred darkens life; love illuminates it.

MARTIN LUTHER KING JR.

My love go if you must; only leave
Your smile to mend my heart,
Your kiss upon my lips to heal my spirit,
Your sweet voice to appease my soul.

SPOON JACKSON
Powder Love, 1992

If I thought black women belonged to black men,
I would have to be upset when I saw a black man
with a white woman. You remember people see-
ing black men with white women and saying,
"We're not going to let our men. . ." I say, hey,
these men don't belong to us. They belong to
themselves.

We need to stop thinking in terms of posses-
siveness, with men thinking, "That's my woman,"
and women thinking, "Those are my men." You
can't have a relationship with people who think
about you that way. What's the difference between
that and, "That's my slave"? . . . We reject it when
white people say, "Those are my niggers," but we
will take the same thought and say, "You are my
woman." It doesn't make sense.

NIKKI GIOVANNI, 1981

One thing . . . that we need to do is focus on people who are really interested in having black to black relationships and leave the other folks alone since they are adults and haven't asked us for help. . . . [W]e don't need to be giving our energy to relationships between black men and white women and vice versa. But a lot of people get caught up in this and this points to some deeper psychological problems involving self-esteem and envy. Well, a person who is coming out of this motivation is probably not going to have a very healthy relationship with anybody.

ERSKINE PETERS, 1992

Black love is Black wealth. . . .

NIKKI GIOVANNI
Poem of a Distant Childhood

You love like a coward. Don't take no steps at all. Just stand around and hope for things to happen outright. Unthankful and unknowing like a hog under a acorn tree. Eating and grunting with your ears hanging over your eyes, and never even looking up to see where the acorns are coming from.

ZORA NEALE HURSTON, 1949

Love does not begin and end the way we think it does. Love is a battle, love is a war; love is a growing up. No one in the world — in the entire world — knows more — knows Americans better or, odd as this may sound, loves them more than the American Negro. This is because he has had to watch you, outwit you, deal with you, and bear you, and sometimes even bleed and die with you, ever since we got here . . . since both of us, black and white, got here — and this is the wedding. Whether I like it or not, or whether you like it or not, we are bound together forever. We are part of each other. What is happening to every Negro in this country at any time is also happening to you.

JAMES BALDWIN, 1961

You can hide the fire, but what about the smoke?

ANONYMOUS

I will be black light as you lie against me
I will be heavy as August over your hair
our rivers flow from the same sea
and I promise to leave you again
full of amazement and our illuminations
dealt through the short tongues of color
or the taste of each other's skin as it hung
from our childhood mouths.

When we meet again
will you put your hands upon me
will I ride you over our lands
will we sleep beneath trees in the rain?
You shall get young as I lick your stomach
hot and at rest before we move off again
you will be white fury in my navel
I will be sweeping night.

AUDRE LORD, 1992

I'd like to tell you a little story now.
Ladies, if you got a man, husband,
    whether you want to call him,
And he don't do exactly like you think he
    should,

20

Don't cut him because you can't raise him
    up again.
Don't hurt him, treat him nice.
And fellas, I wanna say to you,
If you got a wife, a woman, or whatever
    you wanna call her,
(And) She don't do exactly like you think
    she should,
Don't go upside her head,
That don't do but one thing,
That make her a little smarter
She won't let you catch her next time.
So all you do is talk to her softly,
    real sweet, you know,
And you tell her, I know you'll do better.

B.B. KING
(Written by Plummer Davis and Jules Taub)

With children no longer the universally accepted
reason for marriage, marriages are going to have
to exist on their own merits.

ELEANOR HOLMES NORTON, 1970

Build with lithe love. With love like lion
    eyes
With love like morningrise,
With love like black, our black.

GWNEDOLYN BROOKS
The Sermon on Warpland, 1968

One my *loa*
    snake shine
call her mercy
    like my sex
she circles triangular
    figure eights
'round men's necks.
Grass rooted
    ancestor
    corn spirit
    wet my lips
she slow move
    fast move
    'cross flat wood floors.

ALLISON FRANCIS
Mercy Me, 1992

4

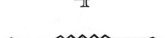

Fight the Power

POLITICS AND BLACKNESS

The dark world is going to submit to its present treatment just as long as it must and not one moment longer.

W.E.B. DU BOIS, 1920

Power in defense of freedom is greater than power in behalf of tyranny.

MINISTER MALCOLM X, 1963

Nonviolent action, the Negro saw, was the way to supplement, not replace, the process of change. It was the way to divest himself of passivity without arraying himself in vindictive force.

MARTIN LUTHER KING JR., 1964

Barking saves biting.

ANONYMOUS

Nonviolence is the answer to the crucial political and moral questions of our time: the need for man to overcome oppression and violence.

Man must evolve for all human conflict a method which rejects revenge, aggression and retaliation. The foundation of such a method is love.

MARTIN LUTHER KING JR., 1963

Sharp ax better'n big muscle.

ANONYMOUS

Let me say straight out that I don't believe in non-violence. . . . I say if a man hits you, you sometimes must hit back. If a sadist comes to your home and threatens your family, you may have to kill him.

Each man has the right, a responsibility, to defend his own life. Freedom is unfortunately, sometimes the freedom to use violence — only after you've first been attacked in some way. But prejudice isn't violence. I'm not saying bigotry isn't rotten. But the line between the man who pulls a gun on me and the bigot who pulls a prejudice against me is a thick line. And if we handle them both the same way, we're trading liberty for the jungle.

JESSE OWENS, 1970

Field Mouse lay still when Sparrow-hawk sail.

ANONYMOUS

Let the Afro-American depend on no party, but on himself for his salvation. Let him continue to education, character, and above all, put money in his purse. When he has a dollar in his pocket and many more in the bank, he can move from injustice and oppression and no one to say him nay. When he has money, and plenty of it, parties and races will become his servants.

IDA B. WELLS, 1892

We have no permanent friends, no permanent enemies, just permanent interests.

REP. WILLIAM L. CLAY, 1971

It's not the man, it's the plan. It's not the rap, it's the map.

OSSIE DAVIS, 1971

[T]he "white supremists" (sic) insist that Negroes are a biologically inferior race and as such must be relegated to an inferior social, economic and political status. . . . The "black supremists" would have us believe that Negroes are "God's chosen people." Beneath the surface these two extreme racial supremists have more in common with each other than they have with the racial group they ostensibly seek to make supreme. Both profit by ignorance and intolerance. . . .

WILLARD S. TOWNSEND, 1944

One-eyed mule cain't be handled on the blind side.

ANONYMOUS

This is a highly complex world. It can be moved by neither blackness nor beauty. It can only be moved by people who know how to handle power. And powerlessness for black people is more of a deterrent to our freedom and our direction than our blackness. In this kind of a world, being black and being beautiful means nothing unless you are black and powerful.

PROF. JOHN HENRIK CLARK, 1971

If you're going to play the game properly, you'd better know every rule.

REP. BARBARA JORDAN, 1975

You'd see more of de mink if he know'd where de yard dog sleep.

ANONYMOUS

Revolution begins with the self, in the self. The individual, the basic revolutionary unit, must be purged of poison and lies that assault the ego and threaten the heart, that hazard the next larger unit — the couple or pair, that jeopardize the still larger unit — the family or cell, that put the entire movement in peril.

TONI CADE BAMBARA, 1969

Who knows when some slight shock, disturbing the delicate balance between social order and thirsty aspiration, shall send the skyscrapers in our cities toppling.

RICHARD WRIGHT, 1940

The nuclear bomb is an equal opportunity destroyer.

REP. RON DELLUMS

[Politics] in the United States . . . is a beautiful fraud that has been imposed on the people for years, whose practitioners exchange gilded promises for the most valuable thing their victims own, their votes.

REP. SHIRLEY CHISHOLM

5

For Together We Stand

BLACKNESS AND BLACK UNITY

Say it Loud: "I'm Black and I'm Proud!"

JAMES BROWN, 1968

Negro blood is sure powerful — because just one drop of black blood makes a colored man. One drop — you are a Negro! . . . Black is powerful.

LANGSTON HUGHES, 1953

I am a black American. Period. The rest is of no consequence to me. Afro-American, African American, whatever. I believe that if I remain a black American I force all others to become and claim their other Americanisms. They are white Americans, Irish Americans, Jewish Americans, or whatever hyphens they would like to use. The noun is "black"; American is the adjective.

NIKKI GIOVANNI, 1993

Please stop using the word "Negro". . . . We are the only human beings in the world with fifty-seven varieties of complexions who are classed together as a single racial unit. Therefore, we are really truly colored people, and that is the only name in the English language which accurately describes us.

MARY CHURCH TERRELL, 1949

Jay bird don't rob his own nes'.

ANONYMOUS, 19th Century

The most demeaning racial utterances against black people I have ever heard firsthand have come out of the mouths of black people. At least white people who were racist would usually wait until I wasn't around. . . . If a white person had innocently shared with me what some black people have innocently shared with me, I would have gone down swinging . . . most white people can't touch black people when it comes to prejudice against black people. White people just wrote the book on it. It is the black people who have perfected the technique in everyday practice. Some white people bend over backward to make black people feel comfortable. And black people will take anything from them, but authority. It's not a fact unless black people hear it from very thin lips. It's not real unless a white person has confirmed it.

RALPH WILEY, 1991

You got eyes to see and wisdom not to (see).

ANONYMOUS, Texas
(An injunction to the slaves not to
tell on one another.)

No one in the wide world is handicapping the Negro, the sleeping Negro has handicapped and is still handicapping himself and not until he realizes the danger of this self-inflicted burden shall he find the way to the post that marks the path to success. I have asserted that you are your own handicappers in the race of life — you supply and strengthen the source of "drawback." If you think this assertion misleading, I am asking you to enquire of yourselves individually: "Have I ever begrudged, despised, slander[ed], treat[ed] unkindly or spoken ill of my brother simply because he is of my own race?" And I know well the answer shall be in the affirmative.

MARCUS GARVEY, 1914

[The Negro past is] of rope, fire, torture, castration, infanticide, rape; death and humiliation; fear by day and night, fear as deep as the marrow of the bone; doubt that he was worthy of life, since everyone around him denied it; sorrow for his women, for his kinfolk, for his children, who needed his protection, and whom he could not protect; rage, hatred and murder, hatred for white men so deep that it often turned against him and his own, and made all love, all trust, all joy impossible.

JAMES BALDWIN, 1963

When the Negro learns what manner of man he is spiritually, he will wake up all over. He will stop playing white, even on the stage. He will rise in the majesty of his own soul. He will glorify the beauty of his own brown skin. He will stop thinking white and go to thinking straight and living right. He will realize that wrong-reaching, wrong-bleaching, and wrong-mixing have "most nigh ruint him" and he will redeem his body and rescue his soul from the bondage of that death.

NANNIE HELEN BURROUGHS, 1927

Black is beautiful.

ANONYMOUS

The topic of black-on-black crime upsets me to no end. To think that for so many years we were oppressed by the white man and when equality is on the horizon, our own race erupts in total chaos. . . .

MICHELLE G. (age 17), 1990

God had instituted a test for those who were seeking admission to heaven: each person had to ask God a question He could not answer before getting in. Several whites tried to stump God with difficult questions, but failed. A Negro man approached, and with some boredom God asked what his question was. The Negro asked: "When will Negroes get together?" Without hesitation God said, "Come right on in, son!"

ANONYMOUS, 19th Century

Before a group can enter the open society, it must first close ranks.

KWAME TOURE AND
CHARLES VERNON HAMILTON, 1968

[After the Watts riots] I experienced that strange combination of power and powerlessness that you feel when the actions of another black person affect your own life, simply because you are both black. For I knew that the actions of people I did not know had become my responsibility as surely as if the black folk in Watts had been my relatives. . . .

HENRY LEWIS GATES JR., 1993

One rain won't make a crop.

ANONYMOUS, Deep South

I here proceeded to make some inquiries of him [Nat Turner] — after assuring him of the certain death that awaited him, and that concealment would only bring destruction of the innocent as well as [the] guilty of his color — if he knew of any extensive or concerted plan [to carry out the insurrection against whites]. His answer was, "I do not." When I questioned him as to the insurrection in North Carolina happening about the same time, he denied any knowledge of it; and when I looked him in the face as though I would search his inmost thoughts, he replied, "I see, sir, you doubt my word; but can you not think the same ideas, and strange appearances about this time in the heavens, might prompt others as well as myself to this undertaking?"

REVOLUTIONARY NAT TURNER TO HIS COURT-
APPOINTED ATTORNEY, THOMAS R. GRAY
(on what prompted the 1830 slave
insurrection in Southampton, VA)

One finger won't catch fleas.

ANONYMOUS

I am so much more than the one wronged, misunderstood, underestimated, derided, or ignored by whites. I am more than the one who has struggled against this oppression and indifference; more than a descendent of slaves now claiming freedom. . . .

Who am I, then? Foremost, I am a child of God, created in his image, imbued with his spirit, endowed with his gifts, set free by his grace. The most important challenges and opportunities that confront me derive not from my social condition, but rather my human condition. I am a husband, a father, a son, a teacher, an intellectual, a Christian, a citizen. In none of these roles is my race irrelevant, but neither can racial identity alone provide much guidance for my quest to adequately discharge my responsibilities. The particular features of my social condition, the external givens, merely set the stage of my life, they do not provide a script. That script must be internally generated, it must be a product of a reflective deliberation about the meaning of this existence for which no political or ethnic program could ever substitute.

GLENN C. LOURY, 1993

6

Us'n Them

BLACKNESS VS. WHITENESS (ET AL.)

We Americans have a chance to become someday a nation in which all racial stocks and classes
can exist in their own selfhoods, but meet on a
basis of respect and equality and live together,
socially, economically, and politically. We can
become a dynamic equilibrium, a harmony of
many different elements, in which the whole will
be greater than all its parts and greater than any
society the world has seen before. It can still
happen.

SHIRLEY CHISHOLM, ca. 1970

White people in this country will have quite
enough to do in learning how to accept and love

themselves and each other, and when they have achieved this — which will not be tomorrow and may very well be never — the Negro problem will no longer exist, for it will no longer be needed.

JAMES BALDWIN, 1963

Crow and corn cain't grow in de same field.

ANONYMOUS, 19th Century

In all things that are purely social we [black and white] can be as separate as the fingers, yet one as the hand in all things essential to mutual progress.

BOOKER T. WASHINGTON, 1895

Tain't much difference betwixt a hornet and a yella-jacket when dey both under your clothes.

ANONYMOUS, 19th Century

The ultimate weakness of violence is that it is a descending spiral, begetting the very thing it seeks to destroy. Instead of diminishing evil, it multiplies it. Through violence you murder the hater, but you do not murder hate. In fact, violence merely increases hate. . . . Returning violence for violence only multiplies violence, adding deeper darkness to a night already devoid of stars. Darkness cannot drive out darkness; only light can do that.

MARTIN LUTHER KING JR.

De rabbit dat sleep in de groundhog's hole needn't 'spec' to have nice dreams.

ANONYMOUS, ca. 19th Century

The relation between the white and colored people of this country is the great, paramount, imperative, and all-commanding question for this age and the nation to solve.

FREDERICK DOUGLASS, 1863

Sometimes the runt pig beats the whole litter growing.

ANONYMOUS

We must find an alternative to violence. The eye-for-an-eye philosophy leaves everybody blind.

MARTIN LUTHER KING JR.

Blacks wake up soon; whites wake up early.

ANONYMOUS, Buffalo, NY

[B]lack women . . . are trained from childhood to become workers, and expect to be financially self-supporting for most of their lives. They know they will have to work, whether they are married or single; work to them, unlike to white women, is not a liberating goal, but rather an imposed lifelong necessity.

GERDA LERNER, 1972

As a part of my argument for education for Negroes I used the incident as illustration that most white people looked upon every Negro, regardless of his appearance, modulated tones that reflected some culture and training, as a servant. . . .

CHARLOTTE BROWN

A white man will recognize a smart Negro but he won't tell the Negro; he'll tell some other white man.

ANONYMOUS

The rules that existed for all those years of slavery still haven't been broken down a hundred percent, socially and mentally. Until you, white man, can see me walk into a restaurant and not stare any more than you would if another white walked in, the house of prejudice still stands. And until you, black man, can walk into that restaurant and not expect to see stares — and not care if you do — you're still sharecropping.

JESSE OWENS, 1970

A white man knows when you're right; he sees, but acts like he don't.

ANONYMOUS

Black is beautiful when it is a slum kid studying to enter college, when it is a man learning new skills for a new job, or a slum mother battling to give her kids a chance for a better life. But white is beautiful, too, when it helps change society to make our system work for black people also. White is ugly when it oppresses blacks — and so is black ugly when black people exploit other blacks. No race has a monopoly on vice or virtue, and the worth of an individual is not related to the color of his skin.

WHITNEY MOORE YOUNG JR., 1969

7

Only the Strong Survive

COURAGE

Now they can call you names — and they will. But you just ignore it. You know you're somebody. Most of them don't have a pot to piss in. But if one hits you, I want you to haul off and smack the shit out him. Do you hear me? We can't have any of that. If they ever get the notion you're a punching bag, you'll be one for the rest of your life. You've got to learn how to stand up for yourself and defend yourself.

RANDALL KENAN, 1989

You're either part of the solution or you're part of the problem.

ATTRIBUTED TO ELDRIDGE CLEAVER, 1968

If a man hasn't discovered something that he will die for, he isn't fit to live.

MARTIN LUTHER KING JR., 1963

It's easy 'nough to titter w'en de stew
   is smokin' hot.
But hits mighty ha'd to giggle w'en dey's
   nuffin' in de pot.

PAUL L. DUNBAR
Philosophy

Look upon your mother, wife and children, and answer God Almighty! And believe this: that it is no more harm for you to kill a man who is trying to kill you than it is for you to take a drink of water when thirsty; in fact, the man who will stand still and let another murder him, is worse than an infidel and, if he has common sense, ought not to be pitied.

DAVID WALKER, 1829

The ultimate measure of a person is not where they stand in moments of comfort and convenience, but where they stand at times of challenge and controversy.

MARTIN LUTHER KING JR.

Let a new earth rise. Let another
    world be born. Let a bloody
peace be written in the sky. Let a second
    generation
full of courage issue forth;
let a people loving free —
dom come to growth.

MARGARET WALKER
For My People, 1942

The common foe of the whole human race is war, because war is a heinous and blasphemous negation of all right human relations. Nevertheless, a nation is often drawn into this disaster, and then every citizen becomes a guardian of his country's life. Then loyalty demands every sacrifice save that of honor.

LESLIE PINCKNEY HILL, 1944

Ain't nothin to it but to do it.

ANONYMOUS, Buffalo, NY

"Listen baby, people do funny things. Specially us. The cards are stacked against us and just trying to stay in the game, stay alive and in the game, makes us do funny things. Things we can't help. Things that make us hurt one another. We don't even know why. But look here, don't carry it inside and don't give it to nobody else. Try to understand it, but if you can't, just forget it and keep yourself strong, man."

TONI MORRISON, 1977

Life goes on, buried in pain for those who wait; swollen with haughtiness and arrogance for those who fear.

DORA ALONSO, 1973

It may well be that the greatest tragedy of this period of social transition is not the glaring noisiness of the so-called bad people, but the appalling silence of the so-called good people.

MARTIN LUTHER KING JR.

A few of us must be sacrificed in order to get a step further.

CHARLOTTE BROWN, 1921

I felt that one had better die fighting against injustice than to die like a dog or a rat in a trap. I had already determined to sell my life as dearly as possible if attacked. I felt if I could take one lyncher with me, this would even up the score a little bit.

IDA B. WELLS

8

R·E·S·P·E·C·T

EQUALITY AND JUSTICE

True peace is not merely the absence of tension
but the presence of justice and brotherhood.

MARTIN LUTHER KING JR.

There is always a person greater and lesser than
yourself.

ANONYMOUS, Buffalo, NY

The potential for strength, endurance, courage,
inventiveness, and creativity exists in every human being God created. If it doesn't appear, it's

because somebody has trifled with it. If you don't see [these things] in young black men and women today to the extent you think you ought to . . . it's because [they've] been unduly trifled with.

MICHELE WALLACE, 1981

[W]hen legal inequalities pass from the statute books, a rock wall of social discrimination between human beings will long persist in human intercourse. So far as such discrimination is a method of social selection, by means of which the worst is slowly weeded and the best protected and encouraged, such discrimination has justification. But the danger has always been and still persists, that what is weeded out is the Different and not the Dangerous; and what is preserved is the Powerful and not the Best. The only defense against this is the widest human contacts and the acquaintanceships compatible with social safety.

W.E.B. DU BOIS, 1944

It rains, and every man feels it some day.

ANONYMOUS, Deep South

I think that non-violent resistance is the most po-
tent weapon available to oppressed people in
their struggle for freedom and human dignity. It
has a way of disarming the opponent. It exposes
his moral defenses. It weakens his morale and at
the same time it works on his conscience. He just
doesn't know how to handle it and I have seen
this over and over again in our struggle in the
South. Now on the question of love or the love
ethic, I think this is so important because hate is
injurious to the hater as well as the hated.

MARTIN LUTHER KING JR., 1963

Waiting on de table is a powerful way to get up a
appetite.

ANONYMOUS

As long as you keep a person down, some part of
you has to be down there to hold him down, so
it means you cannot soar as you otherwise might.

MARIAN ANDERSON, 1957

Bigotry against us because of our skins is sick,
but at least it is out-and-out sickness that every

reasonable person condemns. Bigotry *for* us because of our skins is an insidious emotional tokenism that can quietly widen the breach between black and white, liberal and moderate, young and not so young.

JESSE OWENS, 1970

If we had been allowed to participate in the vital processes of America's national growth, what would have been the textures of our lives, the pattern of our traditions, the routine of our customs, the state of our arts, the code of our laws, the function of our government! We black folk say that America would have been stronger and greater.

RICHARD WRIGHT, 1941

All de justice in de world ain't fastened up in the courthouse.

ANONYMOUS

The rich rob the poor and the poor rob one another.

SOJOURNER TRUTH

Injustice anywhere is a threat to justice everywhere.

MARTIN LUTHER KING JR., 1963

I see that the path of progress has never taken a straight line, but has always been a zigzag course amid the conflicting forces of right and wrong, truth and error, justice and injustice, cruelty and mercy.

KELLY MILLER, 1914

America is woven of many strands; I would recognize them and let them so remain. . . . Our fate is to become one, and yet many.

RALPH ELLISON, 1952

[A]ny human being who is intelligent has the right to defend himself.

MINISTER MALCOLM X, 1963

You can't hold a man down without staying down with him.

ATTRIBUTED TO BOOKER T. WASHINGTON

What do you get with integration? I'll tell you what you get. You get suspected of everything. Every time you earn something, somebody gave it to you. Every time you work hard for something, you're a natural. Every time you show merit, the rules on merit are altered to make them more obtuse.

RALPH WILEY, 1991

[T]he majority of men do not usually act in accord with reason, but follow social pressures, inherited customs and long established, often subconscious, patterns of action. Consequently, race prejudice in America will linger long and may even increase. It is the duty of the black race to maintain its cultural advance, not for itself alone, but for the emancipation of mankind, the realization of democracy and the progress of civilization.

W.E.B. DU BOIS, 1944

But if by some miracle, and all our struggle, the Earth is spared, only justice to every living thing (and everything is alive) will save humankind.

ALICE WALKER

9

It's a Family Affair

FAMILIES

When a man lives a decent life, takes care of his family, and is a contributing member of his community, that's not news. Such a man doesn't get into the headlines. But sometimes I think that sort of everyday achievement should be printed in the newspapers and magazines. . . .

MILT HINTON, 1955

I am not a role model . . . I am paid to wreak havoc on a basketball court. Parents should be role models. Just because I dunk a basketball doesn't mean I should raise your kids.

CHARLES BARKLEY, 1993

CHAPTER NINE

Don't lay it on the cow when the milk gets sour.

ANONYMOUS

[B]lack people in this country . . . must stop drinking, we must stop smoking, we must stop committing fornication and adultery, we must stop gambling and cheating and using profanity, we must stop showing disrespect for our women, we must reform ourselves as parents so we can set the proper example for our children.

MINISTER MALCOLM X, 1963

The greatest positive contribution the race can make a deranged and demoralized civilization will be disciplined parents in upright, democratic homes wherein they shall be taught respect for the laws of God and man, obedience to rightful authority, the universal need of self-sacrifice, responsibility for some worthy service to the family group, and the value of all work well done. . . .

LESLIE PINCKNEY HILL, 1944

On the road to equality there is no better place for blacks to detour around American values than in forgoing its example in the treatment of its women and the organization of its family life.

ELEANOR HOLMES NORTON, 1970

A crooked cornstalk can have a straight ear.

ANONYMOUS

In search of my mother's garden I found my own.

ALICE WALKER, 1974

10

If I Were Your Woman and You Were My Man

MASCULINITY AND FEMININITY

The true worth of a race must be measured by the character of its womanhood. . . .

MARY MC LEOD BETHUNE, 1933

Black womanhood is outraged and humiliated. Black womanhood cries for dignity and restitution and salvation. Black womanhood wants and needs protection, and keeping and holding. Who will assuage her indignation? Who will keep her precious and pure? Who will glorify and proclaim her beautiful image? To whom will she cry rape?

ABBEY LINCOLN, 1966

Men like buses. You miss the first one, it won't be fifteen minutes till the next one roll by.

ANONYMOUS

Rooster makes more racket than de hen what lay de egg.

ANONYMOUS

We, the black women of today, must accept the full weight of a legacy wrought in blood by our mothers in chains. As heirs of a tradition of perseverance and heroic resistance, we must hasten to take our place wherever our people are forging toward freedom.

ANGELA DAVIS, 1971

Woman, if the soul of the nation is to be saved, I believe that you must become its soul.

CORETTA SCOTT KING

In order to function as a slave, the black woman had to be annulled as a woman, that is, as a woman in her historical stance of wardship under the entire male hierarchy. The sheer force of things rendered her equal to her man.

ANGELA DAVIS, 1971

Looks won't do to split rails with.

ANONYMOUS, 19th Century

That man . . . says that women need to be helped into carriages, and lifted over ditches, and to have the best place everywhere. Nobody ever helps me into carriages, over mud puddles, or gives me any best place, and ain't I a woman? . . . I have plowed and planted and gathered into barns, and no man could head me — and ain't I a woman? I could work as much and eat as much as a man (when I could get it), and bear the lash as well — and ain't I a woman? I have borne thirteen children and seen them most all sold off into slavery, and when I cried out with a mother's grief, none but Jesus heard — and ain't I a woman?

SOJOURNER TRUTH, 1865

There are not many males, black or white, who wish to get involved with a woman who's committed to her own development.

ELEANOR HOLMES NORTON, 1970

Mens! You can dress 'em up, but you can't take 'em out.

ANONYMOUS, Buffalo, NY

He's a good, honest man; you don't never hear nobody say nothing about him and no womens. That's hard here in [this town] because the womens treats the mens nice; but it's a small town and the folks likes to talk. . . . I reckon he must go out of town because all you mens is devils.

ANONYMOUS, ca. 1920

Those black males who try to hold women down are expressing in sexist terms the same kinds of expressions in racist terms which they would deny. . . .

JACQUELYNE JACKSON, 1974

The fact that the adult American Negro female emerges as a formidable character is often met with amazement, distaste and even belligerence. It is seldom accepted as an inevitable outcome of the struggle won by survivors, and deserves respect if not enthusiastic acceptance.

MAYA ANGELOU, 1969

I'm a woman. I'm a black woman. I'm a poor woman. I'm a fat woman. I'm a middle-aged woman. And I'm on welfare. In this country if you're any one of those things, you count less as a person. If you're all those things, you just don't count, except as a statistic. I am a statistic.

JOHNNIE TILLMON, 1972

Ships at a distance have every man's wish on board. For some they come in with the tide. For others they sail forever on the horizon, never out of sight, never landing, until the Watcher turns his eyes away in recognition, his dreams mocked to death by time. That is the life of men. Now, women forget all those things they don't want to remember, and remember everything they don't want to forget. The dream is the truth. Then they act and do things accordingly.

ZORA NEALE HURSTON, 1937

A woman ain't never too old to have a boyfriend . . . I tell you the truth, I wants one to come and see me about once a week and pep me up and unruffle me. That's what God made men for.

ANONYMOUS 70-year-old woman

Whoever walked behind anyone to freedom? If we can't go hand-in-hand I don't want to go.

HAZEL SCOTT, 1974

11

Save the Children

OUR YOUTH

A hard head makes a soft behind.

ANONYMOUS, Virginia

The situation of our youth is not mysterious. Children have never been very good at listening to their elders, but they have never failed to imitate them. They must, they have no other models. . . . They are imitating our immorality, our disrespect for the pain of others.

JAMES BALDWIN, 1961

[Our young people] should remember that their source of origin is beyond human beings. And

that even if they don't have any earthly parents
that they should always keep connected with the
divine source from which their parents came
since their parents and no humans are the origin
of being but are rather only vehicles of being. So
the fact is that they are never really powerless
and anyone who teaches this is teaching distor-
tion. It is very important for oppressed people to
be taught this in their earliest years. . . . So we
are never really powerless; it is all a matter of dis-
cerning where your power lies and of deciding
how to get the most value from it.

ERSKINE PETERS, 1992

Do not let yourself be overwhelmed! If you are
wise, strong enough to survive the threatening
atmosphere of the streets, then channel that
same energy into thriving in that same atmosphere
at your school.

BILL COSBY, 1993

And you will understand all too soon
That you, my children of battle, are your
    heroes

CHAPTER ELEVEN

> You must invent your own games and teach
>   us old ones
> How to play

NIKKI GIOVANNI
Poem for Black Boys, 1970

When you're young, the silliest notions seem the greatest achievements.

PEARL BAILEY, 1968

Children's talents to endure stems from their ignorance of alternatives.

MAYA ANGELOU, 1969

Always know that there is unlimited power in a developed mind and a disciplined spirit. If your mind can conceive it and your heart can believe it, you can achieve it. Suffering breeds character; character breeds faith, and in the end, faith will prevail. Armed with this knowledge and a faith in God, you can turn minuses into pluses; you can turn stumbling blocks into stepping stones. It is tough, but your trials will serve to make you strong. Though your enemies will try to break your spirit, you are not the hole in the donut, my son; you are the gold in the ghetto. Keep polishing, keep shining that gold and you will be light in the darkness and heat in cold places. But what's more, you will be a man with integrity, my son.

JESSE JACKSON, 1993

12

Acquainted with de Daybreak

HARD WORK

No race can prosper till it learns that there is as much dignity in tilling a field as in writing a poem.

BOOKER T. WASHINGTON, 1901

De good farmer keeps acquainted with de daybreak.

ANONYMOUS

The principal horror of any system which defines the good in terms of profit rather than in terms of human need to the exclusion of the psychic and emotional components of that need — the principal horror of such a system is that it robs our work of its erotic value, its erotic power and life appeal and fulfillment. Such a system reduces work to a travesty of necessities, a duty by which we earn bread or oblivion for ourselves and those we love. But this is tantamount to blinding a painter and then telling her to improve her work and enjoy the act of painting. It is not only next to impossible, it is also profoundly cruel.

AUDRE LORD, 1992

Nigger dat gets hurt workin oughta show de scars.

ANONYMOUS

Lazy folks' stomachs don't get tired.

ANONYMOUS

The return from your work must be the satisfaction which that work brings you and the world's need of that work. With this, life is heaven, or as near heaven as you can get. Without this — with work which you despise, which bores you, and which the world does not need — this life is hell.

W.E.B. DU BOIS, 1958

Rails split for breakfast'll season de dinner.

ANONYMOUS

It is important and right that all privileges of law be ours, but it is vastly more important that we be prepared for the exercise of these privileges. The opportunity to earn a dollar in a factory just now is worth infinitely more than the opportunity to spend a dollar in an opera house.

BOOKER T. WASHINGTON, 1895

Lookin for work and prayin not to find it.

ANONYMOUS, NORTH CAROLINA

I think I have learned in some degree at least to disregard the old maxim, "Do not get others to do what you can do for yourself." My motto on the other hand is, "Do not do that which others can do as well."

BOOKER T. WASHINGTON

Sleepy fisherman totes a light load home.

ANONYMOUS

All token blacks have the same experience. I have been pointed at as a solution to things that have not begun to be solved, because pointing at us token blacks eases the conscience of millions, and I think this is dreadfully wrong.

LEONTYNE PRICE, 1959

If we so damn lazy how come whitefolks always talkin 'bout how they 'worked like a nigger' every time they breaks a sweat?

ANONYMOUS, Colorado

13

Tell Me Somethin' Good

WISDOM OF THE FOLK

When you clench your fist, no one can put anything in your hand, nor can your hand pick anything up.

ALEX HALEY

Big blanket mek man sleep late.

ANONYMOUS, Creole

Dog have shine teet' him belong to butcher.

ANONYMOUS, Creole

Fowl weary, hawk catch him chicken.

ANONYMOUS, Creole

The way to make a mountain out of a molehill is to keep on adding dirt.

ANONYMOUS, Buffalo, NY

Bull's horns never too heavy for him head.

ANONYMOUS, Creole

No t'ief like see noder t'ief carry long bag.

ANONYMOUS, Creole

One time de mistake, two time a purpose.

ANONYMOUS, Creole

Old britches loves a long coattail.

ANONYMOUS, 19th Century

Distance to de next mile post depend on de mud in de road.

ANONYMOUS, 19th Century

Liquor talk mighty loud when it get loose from de jug.

ANONYMOUS

Hongry Rooster don't cackle when he find a worm.

ANONYMOUS

Can't tell much about a chicken pie till you get through de crust.

ANONYMOUS

Don't sell the bear-skin till you done caught the bear.

ANONYMOUS

Ol' Goose sorta suspicious about the feather bed.

ANONYMOUS

A man that pets a live catfish ain't crowded with brains.

ANONYMOUS

De mocking boid never get outta tune.

ANONYMOUS

Mule dat chew up his own collar be fixing for a sore shoulder.

ANONYMOUS

Sunflower ain't so mighty pretty in the dark.

ANONYMOUS

The wheat crop cain't fool you when it comes to the thrashing.

ANONYMOUS

Dirt shows up quickest on the cleanest cotton.

ANONYMOUS, Texas

Get the candles lighted *before* you blow out the match.

ANONYMOUS, North Carolina

Every eye shut ain't asleep.

ANONYMOUS, North Carolina

The eyebrow is older than the beard.

ANONYMOUS, North Carolina

Set a cracked plate down softly.

ANONYMOUS, North Carolina

Quagmires don't hang out no signs.

ANONYMOUS, North Carolina

A robin's song ain't pretty to a worm.

ANONYMOUS, North Carolina

If you don't have the best of everything, make the best of everything you have.

ANONYMOUS, Buffalo, NY

Keep your dress down and your draws up.

ANONYMOUS, Buffalo, NY

If it don't fit, don't force it.

ANONYMOUS, Buffalo, NY

Give some people an inch and they think they're a ruler.

ANONYMOUS, Buffalo, NY

Keeping up with the Joneses will keep you down.

ANONYMOUS

If you don't succumb to flattery, you can't be crushed by disappointment.

GOV. L. DOUGLAS WILDER, 1993

Money talks, bullshit walks.

ANONYMOUS

Fire don't crack a full pot.

ANONYMOUS, Deep South

Don't waste all your buckshot on one bird.

ANONYMOUS, Colorado

14

The Sacred Fire

ART

And like any artist with no art form, she became
dangerous.

TONI MORRISON, 1974

You got to be ruthless
    to be a poet
        you got to know when to kill
            when you pull the knife

                    and stab

          without mercy
      sometimes you must learn to walk
without ruth

          when you're a poet

just raise your gat and Blast when
you got to
    cries and pleas   must mean nothing
                      when you're a poet
you must begin to appreciate the sounds
    of a slaughter
blood and guts must become to you what
    they are to a vulture
you must be willing to immerse yourself
    in death
    to find the living and kill them
                      if you must
you must walk with the reaper
inside the valley of shadows
to be a poet   you must be unafraid

JAMAL HOLMES
Untitled No. 1

It is the duty of the younger Negro artist . . . to
change through the force of his art that old whis-
pering, "I want to be white," hidden in the aspi-
rations of his people, to, "Why should I want to
be white? I am a Negro — and beautiful!"

LANGSTON HUGHES, 1926

You got to get ugly to sing. Some folks wants to look all pretty — keep a smile — and sing; you can't do that.

ANONYMOUS

Man, if you gotta ask you'll never know.

LOUIS "SATCHMO" ARMSTRONG
(when asked what jazz is)

Lady, if you got to ask you ain't got it.

THOMAS "FATS" WALLER
(when asked to explain rhythm)

The best, authentic black music does not unravel the mysteries, but recalls them, gives them a particular form, a specific setting, attaches the mysteries to familiar words and ideas. Simple lyrics of certain songs follow us, haunt us because the words floating in the music are a way of eavesdropping on the mysteries, of remembering the importance of who we are but also experiencing the immensity of Great Time and Great Space, the Infinite always at play around the edges of our lives.

JOHN EDGAR WIDEMAN, 1984

Gospel music in those days of the early 1930's was really taking wing. It was the kind of music colored people had left behind them down south and they liked it because it was just like a letter from home.

MAHALIA JACKSON, 1966

O black and unknown bards of long ago,
How came your lips to touch the sacred
    fire?
How, in your darkness, did you come to
    know
The power and beauty of the minstrel's
    lyre?

JAMES WELDON JOHNSON
O Black and Unknown Bards, 1917

15

Take Me to the River

DEATH

Ol' Master had this irritating habit a telling these looooong-ass stories 'bout these dreams he used to had. Well, one day he come upon one a his most trickenest old slaves name of Peter-Paul, who was out in the chicken yard, fend to feed the chickens. The ol' whiteman grin and say, "Oooeee, Pete-Paul, I sho did have me a funny dream last night." And ol' Peter-Paul say, he say, "Do tell, Mas'. Do tell."

"'Tend to, Pete-Paul, 'tend to. It happen this-away: Dreamed I found myself up in Nigger Heaven, see, and, Lord, I'm here to tell you right now a sorrier place I ain't seen. Worse looking than this here chicken yard — dirt, sorry clumps a grass here'n there; flies, rubbish, rickety shacks made a driftwood and mud. Thousands a ragged looking niggers crowding the dusty streets. Oooeee, I'm here to tell you, boy, it was one sorry hereafter." And Peter-Paul say, "Well hesh my mouth, Mas', I had me the veriest same dream last night, more or less." And Master, he say, "Whachu mean 'more or less,' Pete-Paul?"

Peter-Paul squint one eye and he say, "Well, sir, I had me a heaven dream, too, 'cept it was Buckra Heaven I went to. Oooo, and you wanna talk 'bout some pretty pearly gates — "

"Well, well — "

"Indeed, sir. Streets a gold, mansions a silver, big ol' pretty green lawns, trees, flowers, lakes and streams — "

"Well now."

"Uh-huh, milk an' honey ev'where you lay your eyes. . . . 'Cept one mos' peculiar thing there, Mas'."

"Whazzat, boy?"

"Whadn't a soul in de place."

ANONYMOUS, Texas, 19th Century

Black folks afraid a dying, but ain't afraid of death. White folks afraid of death, but ain't afraid of dying.

ANONYMOUS, Colorado

Life is better than death, I believe, if only because it is less boring, and because it has fresh peaches in it.

ALICE WALKER

The proudness of a man don't count when his head's cold.

ANONYMOUS, 19th Century

Tomorrow may be de carriage driver's day for plowing.

ANONYMOUS, 19th Century

You never know the length of a snake until its death.

ANONYMOUS, North Carolina

Dead is dead.

ANONYMOUS, Mississippi

16

Free at Last! Free at Last!

FREEDOM

We are involved in a struggle for liberation: liberation from the exploitive and dehumanizing system of racism, from the manipulative control of a corporate society; liberation from the constrictive norms of "mainstream" culture, from the synthetic myths that encourage us to fashion ourselves rashly from without (reaction) rather than from within (creation).

TONI CADE BAMBARA, 1967

Human freedom is a complex, difficult — and private — thing. If we can liken life, for a moment, to a furnace, the freedom is the fire which burns away illusion.

JAMES BALDWIN, 1963

To die for the revolution is a one-shot deal; to live for the revolution means taking on the more difficult commitment of changing our day-to-day life patterns.

FRANCES M. BEAL, 1970

When I found I had crossed the line [to freedom], I looked at my hands to see if I was the same person. There was such a glory over everything.

HARRIET TUBMAN

No man can put a chain around the ankle of his fellow man without at last finding the other end fastened around his neck.

FREDERICK DOUGLASS, 1883

The cost of liberty is less than the price of repression.

W.E.B. DU BOIS

As a child, whenever I was apt to become a bit too recalcitrant or downright rebellious, refusing to do something my mother, in her wisdom, thought it to be in my best interest to do, I would, when scolded, reply sullenly, "Well, you know, Mom, it's a free country." And she would inevitably say, "I got news for you: That's the biggest lie that's ever been told. Nothing's free."

GERALD EARLY, 1992

His headstone said
Free at last, Free at last
But death is a slave's freedom
We seek the freedom of free men
And the construction of a world
Where Martin Luther King
        could have lived
        and preached nonviolence.

NIKKI GIOVANNI
The Funeral of Martin Luther King Jr., 1968

You mize well die with the chills as with the fever. (You might as well get killed trying to escape as opposed to remaining a slave and dying in slavery.)

ANONYMOUS, Texas

Oh, freedom! Oh, freedom!
Oh, freedom over me!
And before I'd be a slave, I'll be buried in
    my grave.

ANONYMOUS
Oh, Freedom!

The limits of tyrants are prescribed by the endurance of those whom they oppress.

FREDERICK DOUGLASS

If our people are to fight their way up out of bondage we must arm them with the sword and the shield and the buckler of pride.

MARY MCLEOD BETHUNE, 1938

I had reasoned this out in my mind, there was two things I had a right to, liberty and death. If I could not have one, I would have the other, for no man should take me alive.

HARRIET TUBMAN

If slavery isn't wrong, nothing is wrong.

ANONYMOUS, Buffalo, NY

Once the problem of subsistence is met and order is secured, there comes the great moment of civilization: the development of individual personality; the right of variation; the richness of a culture that lies in differentiation. In the activities of such a world, men are not compelled to be white in order to be free: they can be black, yellow or red; they can mingle or stay separate. ... The hope of civilization lies not in exclusion, but inclusion of all human elements; we find the richness of humanity not in the Social Register, but in the City Directory; not in great aristocracies, chosen people and superior races, but in the throngs of disinherited and underfed men.

W.E.B. DU BOIS, 1944

Different strokes for different folks.

ANONYMOUS

Whence all this passion toward conformity anyway? — diversity is the word. Let man keep his many parts, and you'll have no tyrant states. ... It's "winner take nothing" that is the great truth of our country or any country. Life is to be lived, not controlled; and humanity is won by continuing to play in the face of certain defeat. Our fate is to become one, and yet many — this is not prophecy, but description.

RALPH ELLISON, 1952

One monkey don't stop no show.

ANONYMOUS

We lock ourselves up
Not because of the bars and steel
That surround us
Not because life doesn't bend
To our every whim.

But because of the projections
We place on our worlds
The judgments, the "I can'ts"
The thinking the world owes us
A living
The trying to please everyone
While not pleasing ourselves.

By seeking the beauty on the outside
That is surely within

For prisons are created internally
And found everywhere.

SPOON JACKSON
Beauty in Cell Bars, 1992

Jails and prisons are designed to break human
beings, to convert the population into specimens
in a zoo — obedient to our keepers but dangerous to each other.

ANGELA DAVIS, 1974

Like a fawn from the arrow,
    startled and wild,
A woman swept by it
    bearing a child;
In her eye was the night
    of a settled despair,
And her brow was o'ershaded
    with anguish and care.

She was nearing the river —
    in reaching the brink,
She heeded no danger,
    she paused not to think;

For she is a mother —
   her child is a slave —
And she'll give him his freedom,
   or find him a grave!

FRANCES ELLEN WATKINS
Eliza Harris

The concept of rising against oppression through physical contact is stupid and self-defeating. It exalts brawn over brain. It exalts a man or woman's body over the mind. And the most enduring contributions made to civilization have not been made by brawn, they have been made by brain.

BENJAMIN HOOKS, 1981

It's easy to be independent when you've got money. But to be independent when you haven't got a thing — that's the Lord's test.

MAHALIA JACKSON, 1966

The whole history of the progress of human liberty shows that all concessions yet made to her august claims have been born of earnest struggle. . . . If there is no struggle, there is no progress.

Those who profess to favor freedom, and yet deprecate agitation, are men who want crops without plowing the ground, they want rain without thunder and lightning. They want the ocean without the awful roar of its many waters. The struggle may be a moral one, or it may be a physical one, or it may be both. But it must be a struggle. Power concedes nothing without demand; it never has and it never will.

FREDERICK DOUGLASS, 1857

17

In the Upper Room

SPIRITUALITY

A philosophy of life is something that you work with periodically. It's never perfect, even if you developed it yourself! It's only perfect perhaps for the moment and in its generality. But life is not constant, and so as life changes one's philosophy should change too. That doesn't mean that you have to dump everything you've been living by; it only means that you adapt and re-adapt if necessary.

ERSKINE PETERS, 1992

Old Satan loads his cannon with big watermelons.

ANONYMOUS

There is no place in black theology for a colorless God in a society when people suffer precisely because of their color.

DR. JAMES H. CONE, 1971

I am a Muslim and . . . my religion makes me be against all forms of racism. It keeps me from judging any man by the color of his skin. It teaches me to judge him by his deeds and his conscious behavior. And it teaches me to be for the rights of all human beings, but especially the Afro-American human being, because my religion is a natural religion, and the first law of nature is self-preservation.

MINISTER MALCOLM X, 1965

If the concept of God has any validity or use, it can only be to make us larger, freer and more loving. If God cannot do this, then it is time we got rid of Him.

JAMES BALDWIN, 1963

Ugly man don't fool with de looking glass.

ANONYMOUS

What's the point of telling a poor man he might go to hell? He done had hell here; if he gets hell, it'll just be hell all the way through for him. Ain't no point in paying a preacher; ain't nothing he can do for you. What you gets, you got to work for yourself.

ANONYMOUS, ca. 1920

'Twant me, 'twas the Lord. I always told Him, "I trust you. I don't know where to go or what do, but I expect you to lead me." And he always did.

HARRIET TUBMAN, 1868

I refuse to accept the idea that the "isness" of man's present nature makes him morally incapable of reaching up for the "oughtness" that forever confronts him.

MARTIN LUTHER KING JR., 1964

Trouble follows a sin as sure as a fever follows a chill.

ANONYMOUS

One and God make a majority.

FREDERICK DOUGLASS

Old Satan loves a big crowd.

ANONYMOUS

Someday the sun is going to shine down on me in some faraway place.

MAHALIA JACKSON

Unearned suffering is redemptive.

MARTIN LUTHER KING JR.

I have the audacity to believe that people everywhere can have three meals a day for their bodies, education and culture for their minds, and dignity, equality and freedom for their spirits. I believe that what self-centered men have torn down men other-centered can build up. I still believe that one day mankind will bow before the altars of God and be crowned triumphant over war and bloodshed, and non-violent redemptive goodwill proclaim the rule of the land.

MARTIN LUTHER KING JR.
(on receiving the Nobel Peace Prize)

About the Editor

Winner of the O. Henry and the *Kenyon Review* Award for Literary Excellence for the story "The Kind of Light That Shines on Texas," Reginald McKnight is the recipient of a Thomas J. Watson Foundation Fellowship and a 1991 National Endowment for the Arts Grant for Literature. His first collection of short stories, *Moustapha's Eclipse*, was awarded the 1988 Drue Heinz Literature Prize. McKnight is also the author of the critically acclaimed novel *I Get On the Bus*, and the short story collection *The Kind of Light That Shines on Texas*. He is an associate professor of English at Carnegie Mellon University and lives in Pittsburgh, Pennsylvania.

Bibliographic Index

The information in this index allows the reader to locate the contributions of authors within the text and to further explore their writing. Applicable publisher permissions follow the index.

Brown, James (1930–) ("Godfather of Soul,") Rhythm & blues and soul singer; composer who achieved great notoriety mainly between the 1950s and 1970s ("I Feel Good," 1964, "Living in America," 1989), 29

Burroughs, Nannie Helen (1879–1961) School founder, educator, civil rights activist, feminist, religious leader, author (*Making Your Community Christian*; *World of Light and Life Found Here and There*, 1948), 33

Chisholm, Shirley (1924–) first black woman to be elected to the U.S. Congress (1968–82). Founder and Chairperson of the National Political Congress of Black Women (*Unbought and Unbossed* [autobiography] 1970), 28, 38

Clark, John Henrick (1915–) Educator, writer, reviewer, teacher, historian; 27

Clay, William L., Sr. (1931–) Congressman who opened many unions for blacks; 25

Cleaver, (Leroy) Eldridge (1935–) Militant, activist, writer (*Soul on Ice*, 1968), 15, 44

Cone, Dr. James H., Clergyman, professor, author; 95

Cosby, Bill (William H., Jr.) (1937–) Comedian, actor, director, philanthropist, educator, writer (*Fatherhood*, 1987; "Uptown Saturday Night"; "The Cosby Show"), 65

and organizational leadership (*Autobiography of an Ex-Colored Man* [published anonymously] 1912; *God's Trombones*, 1927), 81

Jones, Gayl (1949–) Poet, writer, playwright, educator; professor of English and Afro-American Studies, University of Michigan, 1

Jordan, Barbara (Charline), Lawyer, educator, politician, congressional representative; 27

Kenan, Randall, Author (*A Visitation of Spirits*, 1989; *Let the Dead Bury Their Dead*, 1992), 9, 44

King, B.B. (Blues Boy) (Riley B. King) (1925–) Blues guitarist and singer who is recognized as a principle figure in the development of rhythm and blues and from whose style leading popular musicians drew inspiration. (*The Arrival of B.B. King* [biography] by Charles Sawyer, 1980), 21

King, Coretta Scott, (1927–) President and Chief Executive Officer of the Martin Luther King Jr. Center for Non-Violent Social Change, Inc. in Atlanta. Ms. King is also the Chair of the Martin Luther King Jr. Federal Holiday Commission; 6, 59

King, Martin Luther, Jr. (1929–1968) Eloquent Baptist minister who led the mass civil rights movement in the U.S. from the mid-1950s until his death by assassination in 1968. Nobel Prize for Peace, 1964; author

Tubman, Harriet (1820–1913) Political activist who escaped slavery in the south to become a leading abolitionist before the Civil War; known as the "Moses" of her people for leading hundreds of escaped slaves along the route of the Underground Railroad. 86, 88, 96

Turner, Nat (1800–1831) Revolutionary bondsman who led the only effective sustained slave revolt (August 1831) in U.S. history. (*The Nat Turner Slave Insurrection* by F. Roy Johnson, 1966), 35

Walker, Alice (1944–) Poet, essayist, writer, publisher of Wild Trees Press. (*The Color Purple* [Pulitzer Prize and American Book Award], 1983), 54, 57, 84

Walker, David (1785–1830) Abolitionist whose pamphlet (1829) urged slaves to fight for their freedom; it was one of the most radical documents of the anti-slavery movement; 45

Walker, Margaret Alexander (1915–) Poet, novelist, educator; Emeritus professor of English at Jackson State University in Mississippi (*For My People*, 1942; *Jubilee*, 1966), 46

Wallace, Michele, Writer (*Black Macho & the Myth of the Superwoman*, 1990; *Invisibility Blues: From Pop to Theory*, 1990), 50

Grateful acknowledgment is made to the following for permission to reprint excerpts from previously published material:

The Classic Wisdom Collection

If you would like a catalog of our fine books and cassettes, contact:

New World Library
58 Paul Drive
San Rafael, CA 94903

Or call toll free: (800) 227-3900